DK FIN
NATURE

How to use this book	2
Mosses and weeds	4
Fungi	6
Grasses and cereals	8
Herbs	10
Flowers	12
Fruits and seeds	14
At the beach	16
Shells	18
In the countryside	20
Animal tracks and homes	22
Mini-beasts	24
Trees	26
In the sky	28
Landscape	30
Glossary and index	32

How to use this book

DK Finders Nature is a fun book to take with you on a trip to a park or the countryside. There are 80 different things to find, from plants and animals to clouds, rivers, and lakes. Here you can find out how each page works and what to do with your sticker stars.

Close-up photographs
Look at each photograph carefully so you know what you have to find.

Fascinating facts
Snippets of information give you the name of each thing you have to find and interesting facts about it.

Sticker boxes
Whenever you spot something in the book, stick one of your stars in the box next to it.

In the sky

Cumulus cloud
You'll see these fluffy clouds high in the sky. They look like cotton.

Storm cloud
Thick storm clouds are dark because no light can pass through them from above.

Lightning
During a storm, electricity in the sky produces flashes of lightning.

Things to remember

1. Never go out exploring alone – always ask an adult to go with you.

2. Be careful when out searching: Never touch wild animals and do not taste plants or fungi since they may be poisonous.

3. Do not pick flowers, leave litter, or do anything that may harm a plant or animal.

4. Remember that many plants and animals can only be seen at particular times of the year.

FULL MOON
Once a month, as long as the sky is clear, you'll see the whole shape of the Moon.

SHOOTING STAR
A shooting star is rare. Look for a moving streak of light in the night sky.

RAINBOW
If the sun is shining while it's raining, the raindrops split the sun's rays into the colors that make up white light – red, orange, yellow, green, blue, indigo, and violet – creating a rainbow.

STARBURST BOXES
Ten of the things have a starburst in the box next to them. These are extra hard to spot. When you see one, stick in one of your ten starbursts.

Glossary
Difficult words are explained in a glossary on page 32.

Index
Use the index on page 32 if you want to look up any of the things quickly.

MOSSES AND WEEDS

DOCK
This weed grows in open grassland and along roadsides. It has large green leaves.

MOSS
Mosses are small, simple plants that do not have flowers. They like shady, damp places.

NETTLE
These weeds have hairy stems and jagged leaves. The bristles will sting your skin and give you a rash, so be careful not to brush against them.

Lichen
Lichen grows on roofs and walls as well as on tree trunks and rocks. It needs a lot of moisture and clean air to grow.

Bramble
These weeds grow as prickly bushes with spiky leaves. Some types of brambles, such as the blackberry bush, have fruit.

Fungi

Never eat any fungi that you find when out exploring.

Honey onion mushroom

This orangy-brown mushroom grows in clusters, or scattered, under pine trees.

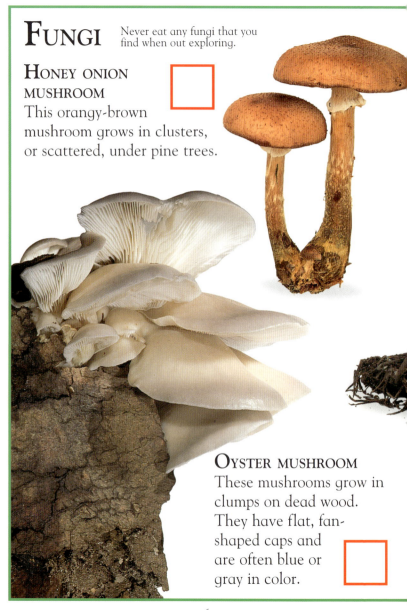

Oyster mushroom

These mushrooms grow in clumps on dead wood. They have flat, fan-shaped caps and are often blue or gray in color.

Fly agaric

These poisonous fungi were once used to make fly poison. They have bright red caps with white spots.

Slippery jack

The Slippery Jack has a slimy brown cap and a ring around its stem. It grows mainly in woodland.

Puffball

This fungus is named after the clouds of tiny, seedlike spores that puff out of its top when anything touches it.

GRASSES AND CEREALS

QUACK GRASS
Quack grass has long,
creeping roots. It
spreads quickly and
attacks fields of crops.

BARLEY
This cereal
is grown for
animal feed. It is
also used to
make beer.

OATS
Oats are grown as
crops, but they also
grow wild. Unlike
barley and rye grains,
each oat grain grows
separately at
the end of
a stem.

Rye

The dark grains of
this cereal are used
to make rye bread
and whiskey. Rye is
also used as an
animal feed.

Wheat

Several varieties of
wheat are grown for
flour. Wheat flour is
used to make pasta,
bread, cakes, and
many other foods.

Herbs

Thyme
Thyme has tiny, strongly scented leaves. Some varieties have lilac flowers.

Bay
This herb has large, tough leaves with a strong aroma. It grows as a small tree or bush.

Dill
This plant is related to the carrot. The leaves are long, fine, and feathery. The aroma is delicate but distinctive.

Basil
Basil has bright green, pointed leaves and a spicy scent. It is a member of the mint family, and likes plenty of sunshine.

Rosemary
Rosemary grows in warm, dry places. Its leaves are very small and spiky.

Borage
This herb has hairy stems, blue flowers, and cucumber-scented oval leaves.

Flowers

Primrose
This plant grows in open grassland and woodland. It has yellow flowers with short stems, and soft, hairy leaves.

Forget-me-not
The forget-me-not is a symbol of faithful love. Its flowers can be either bright blue or white.

Daffodil
Daffodils belong to the narcissus family. The trumpet-centered flowers appear in spring.

Sunflower
These tall yellow flowers are grown as crops for the oil in their seeds. Look out for fields of them in summer.

Periwinkle
These spring flowers are blue or white and have trailing evergreen leaves.

Poppy
Wild poppies often grow in fields and alongside roads. They flower in summer.

Fruits and seeds

Never eat wild fruits, nuts, or seeds.

Acorns
Acorns are the fruits of the oak tree. They appear in the fall, and grow in woody cups at the ends of branches.

Rose hips
Rose hips are the fruits of the rose. They grow after the rose flower has died away.

Pinecones
These woody fruits hold the seeds of evergreen trees. Pinecones can be short and fat or long and thin.

Holly berries
Some types of holly produce clusters of small red berries. Look out for them in winter among spiky holly leaves.

Chestnuts
These nuts are the fruits of the chestnut tree. They grow in prickly cases.

Maple seeds
The seeds of the maple tree grow in winglike cases. They spin around as they fall from the tree.

AT THE BEACH

PUFFIN
Sometimes called a sea parrot, this bird has black and white feathers and orange webbed feet. It nests along coasts.

SEAWEED
Seaweeds are plants that live in the sea. They cling to rocks and are often washed up on the beach.

CRAB
Look for crabs in tide pools during low tide. They have two large claws called pincers for catching food and for self-defense.

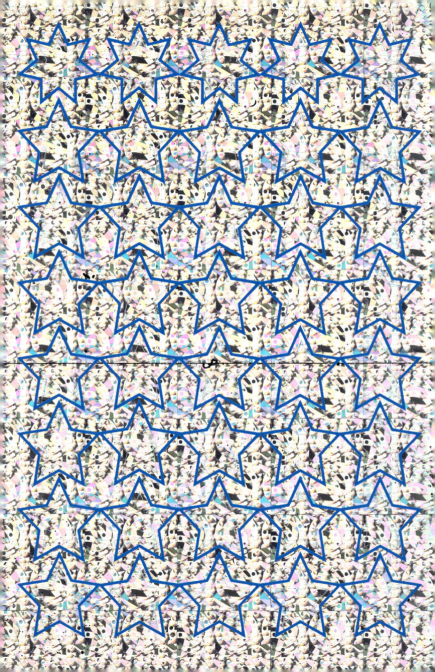

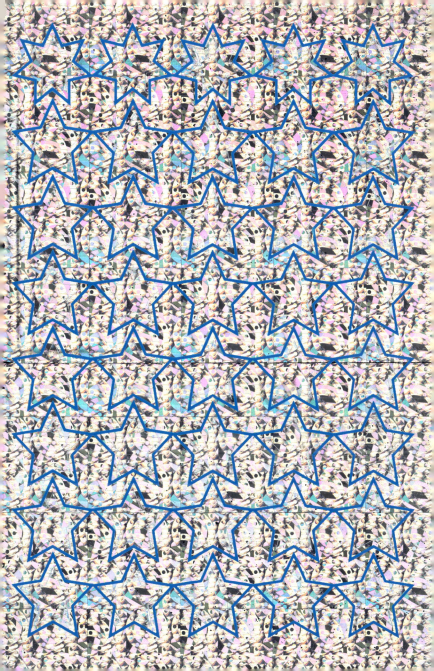

Seagull
Flocks of seagulls fly over the sea looking for fish. They also scavenge for food in towns.

Driftwood
Look for driftwood lying on the beach. Its smooth surface has been worn by the waves.

Starfish
These five-armed animals cannot survive out of the water. Look for them in tide pools.

Sea anemone
These sea creatures attach themselves to rocks. They use their tentacles to paralyze prey.

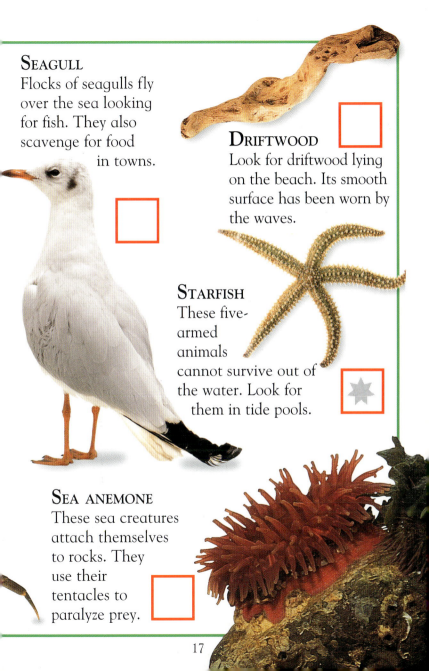

Shells

Scallop
There are lots of types of scallop shells. This Great Scallop, with its serrated edges, is one of the most common.

Limpet
Limpets can be smooth or ribbed. Each shell has a horseshoe-shaped scar inside, where the animal was attached to it.

Razor
These shells are smooth with sharp edges. Razor clams use their sharp shells to help them burrow into sand.

Winkle
There are many different winkles and they vary in size. They can have straight or curved sides.

Whelk
Whelks live in cool waters in sand just offshore. Their spiral shape is long and pointed.

Nautilus
This shell is light, thin, and spiraled. The dark brown mark shows where the sea animal was attached to it.

IN THE COUNTRYSIDE

TOAD
Like frogs, toads live on land and in water. They are usually larger than frogs, and have dry, warty skin.

FOX
Foxes are mostly nocturnal, but you may see one during the day, especially in summer. You can see them in towns as well as the country.

MALLARD
This wild duck lives near inland rivers and lakes. The male mallard has a shiny green head and dark feathers. The female has brown feathers.

Rabbit
Rabbits spend most of their time underground. They are shy, so you'll need to keep quiet to spot one.

Deer
Deer are often seen in woodland areas. They live in groups. The males, called stags, have large antlers.

Squirrel
Squirrels can move easily along tree branches. Red squirrels are much rarer than gray squirrels.

Animal tracks and homes

Bird tracks
Look for bird tracks in sand, mud, or snow. You can often find them early in the day. This gull's tracks show its webbed feet.

Animal tracks
You may see rabbit, fox, or deer tracks in muddy woodland areas. The tracks shown here are a dog's.

Wasp's nest
Papery wasps' nests are often attached to branches or roofs. They are made by the queen wasp from wood and saliva.

Bird's nest
Birds build their nests in trees, buildings, hedges, or even on the ground. Never touch a bird's nest or eggs.

Spider's web
Webs are easy to see early in the morning when they are still covered with dew. Insects become trapped in them and are eaten by the spiders.

Mini-beasts

Ant
You may see lines of marching ants in gardens or woods, carrying food back to the anthill. This is their nest.

Slug
Slugs like damp places where they won't dry out. Look for the slime trails they leave.

Butterfly
You can see all sorts of brightly colored butterflies in summer. Adult butterflies have long, coiled tongues and feed on flower nectar.

Spider
Unlike insects, all spiders have eight legs. They have powerful fangs, which release paralyzing poison into their prey.

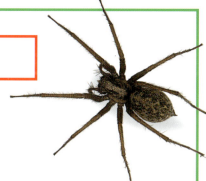

Snail
A snail's soft body is protected by its shell. Its eyes are on the ends of its two longest tentacles.

Ladybug
These beetles feed on tiny insects that live on plants. Their bright red coloring warns predators to stay away.

TREES

Maple
There are many types of maples, but they all have five-pointed leaves. You can see clusters of flowers on a maple tree in spring, just before the leaves come out.

Palm
In addition to growing naturally in hot climates, palm trees are grown inside conservatories all over the world. Some varieties have fruit.

Spruce
This evergreen tree has spiky needles and thin cones. Unlike hard, rough pinecones, spruce cones are bendy and smooth. You may see this species used as a Christmas tree.

Birch
Small, pointed leaves and silvery bark make the birch unique. Look out for catkins (taillike clusters of flowers) in spring.

Oak
There are more than 600 species of oaks. A single tree can produce about 50,000 acorns a year.

In the sky

Cumulus cloud
You'll see these fluffy clouds high in the sky. They look like cotton.

Storm cloud
Thick storm clouds are dark because no light can pass through them from above.

Lightning
During a storm, electricity in the sky produces flashes of lightning.

Full moon
Once a month, as long as the sky is clear, you'll see the whole shape of the Moon.

Shooting star
A shooting star is rare. Look for a moving streak of light in the night sky.

Rainbow
If the sun is shining while it's raining, the raindrops split the sun's rays into the colors that make up white light – red, orange, yellow, green, blue, indigo, and violet – creating a rainbow.

Landscape

River
Rivers can be narrow and fast-flowing or wide, slow, and meandering.

Mountain
Mountains are high hills that were formed by the collision of the Earth's plates.

Sand dune
The low hills of sand along some beaches are called sand dunes. Clumps of grasses grow on them and stop the sand from being blown away.

Cliff

Cliffs are high, steep rocks along some seashores. The action of waves wears away soft rocks and, after thousands of years, harder rocks remain as cliffs.

Lake

A large stretch of water surrounded by land is called a lake. Some lakes are so huge that when you're standing on one side you can't see across to the other.

Waterfall

Waterfalls can be large or small. They are usually found in a youthful river where rocks on the riverbed drop suddenly. The river falls over the steep rocks.

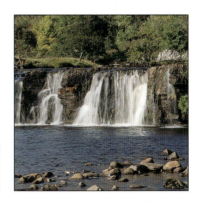

GLOSSARY

Evergreen plants and trees keep their leaves all year round. Evergreen trees are also called coniferous trees.

Fruits are the parts of plants that contain the seeds.

Fungi are organisms such as toadstools, mushrooms, and mold, which grow on other organisms.

Nectar is the sugary liquid inside a flower that insects feed on.

To **paralyze** means to make another animal powerless so that it cannot move.

Plates form the Earth's crust. Long ago, collisions between the plates forced the Earth to fold up and form mountains.

Predators are animals that hunt and eat other animals.

Prey are animals that are hunted and eaten by other animals.

Shells are hard, outer cases that protect some living things.

Species are groups of similar plants or animals that breed together.

Tentacles are long spines used by animals for feeling and moving. Some are armed with stingers.

Weeds are wild plants that grow where they are not wanted.

DK would like to thank the following for their kind permission to reproduce photographs:
t=top, c=center, b=bottom, r=right, l=left

Bruce Coleman Collection: Jane Burton 21tl, Robert P. Carr 27tl; **Brian Cosgrove:** 28t; **Image Bank:** 27bc, Andrea Pistolesi 26cr; **Images Colour Library:** 30tl, 30b, 31br; **Oxford Scientific Films:** David Tipling 21tr; **Photos Horticultural:** M. Warren 26tl, 26bl; **Science Photo Library:** Peter Parviainen 29tr; **Tony Stone Images:** 30tr, 31tr, 31cl, Beryl Bidwell 28clb, Ken Biggs 29tl, Chad Ehlers 28crb, Chris Thomaidis 23cb, Tom Tietz 16tr, Gary Yeowell 29cb.

INDEX

acorns 14
animal tracks 22
ant 24
barley 8
basil 11
bay 10
birch 27
bird tracks 22
bird's nest 23
borage 11
bramble 5
butterfly 24
chestnuts 15
cliff 31
crab 16
cumulus cloud 28
daffodil 12
deer 21
dill 10
dock 4
driftwood 17
fly agaric 7
forget-me-not 12
fox 20
full Moon 29
holly berries 15
honey onion
  mushroom 6
ladybug 25
lake 31
lichen 5
lightning 28
limpet 18
mallard 20
maple 26
maple seeds 15
moss 4
mountain 30
nautilus 19
nettle 4
oak 27
oats 8
oyster
  mushroom 6

palm 26
periwinkle 13
pinecones 14
poppy 13
primrose 12
puffball 7
puffin 16
quack grass 8
rabbit 21
rainbow 29
razor 18
river 30
rose hips 14
rosemary 11
rye 9
sand dune 30
scallop 18
sea anemone 17
seagull 17
seaweed 16
shooting star 29
slippery jack 7
slug 24
snail 25
spider 25
spider's web 23
spruce 26
squirrel 21
starfish 17
storm cloud 28
sunflower 13
thyme 10
toad 20
wasp's nest 22
waterfall 31
wheat 9
whelk 19
winkle 19